From the Heart of a Man

From the Heart of a Man

Words for Lovers and Others

RICK MIZUNO

iUniverse, Inc.
New York Bloomington

FROM THE HEART OF A MAN
WORDS FOR LOVERS AND OTHERS

iUniverse books may be ordered through booksellers or by contacting:

iUniverse
1663 Liberty Drive
Bloomington, IN 47403
www.iuniverse.com
1-800-Authors (1-800-288-4677)

Because of the dynamic nature of the Internet, any Web addresses or links contained in this book may have changed since publication and may no longer be valid. The views expressed in this work are solely those of the author and do not necessarily reflect the views of the publisher, and the publisher hereby disclaims any responsibility for them.

ISBN: 978-1-4401-1467-0 (sc)
ISBN: 978-1-4401-1470-0 (ebook)

Printed in the United States of America

iUniverse rev. date: 1/5/09

Rick Mizuno Productions
P.O. Box 50112
Oxnard, CA 93031
Web site: www.rickmizuno.com
E-mail: look@rickmizuno.com

Dedicated to the one

Who touched my heart… like no other

Who moved my soul… like no other

Who stirred my emotions… like no other

Who awakened me… like no other

These expressions, like no other, are for the lover in my dreams

There is Faith, Hope and Love
… The greatness of these is, Love

I Corinthians 13:13

Foreword
by Jan King

There are those rare people who have the extraordinary ability to live so fully in the moment that they can absorb all aspects of it into their consciousness. Rick Mizuno not only has that ability, but he has the talent to take those moments and allow his readers to feel what he is feeling. This is what he has accomplished so beautifully in *From the Heart of a Man*.

Rick paints a canvas of love, life and loss with the precision of an Old Master. The words flow directly from the soul of a true Renaissance man; a musician, an artisan and a dreamer whose story has been woven from his own personal experience as well as from his observations of others. *From the Heart of a Man* is a sensual journey written by a poet whose written words evoke vibrant images and deep feelings with every stroke of his pen.

Rick has chosen illustrations for his book that are fluid in nature, perfectly complimenting the lyrical quality of his words. *From the Heart of a Man* is truly from the heart of a man who possesses a sensitivity to love and to express love that is nothing less than amazing. It is a very special journey written by a very special man.

Jan King is a conference speaker and the author of *"It's a Girl Thing"*, *"It's a Mom Thing"*, the international best-seller *"Hormones from Hell"* and many other books. She has appeared on the Today show, Jenny Jones, and other national TV talk shows. www.jankingauthor.com

Arlean Mizuno – *Mom*
Marcielle Brandler – *Advice*
Martha Castillo – *Inspiration*
Janine Haydel – *Encouragement*
JJ Kenny – *Motivation*
Natasha Madison – *Affirmation*
Josefa Salinas – *Insight*

My children:
Myeshia, Trashonda, Mia, Rickey
Unconditional love

John and Marsha Silva
More than best friends… family

Kelly Thacher
Editor, critic, coach and friend

Cover Concept
Rick Mizuno

Technical Support
Rickey Mizuno II
www.rmizu.com

Photographer
Corey Wright
www.coreywrightphoto.com

Life Coach
Trashonda Malbrough
www.soundmind4you.com

Interior Artwork
Manuel Bernal
&
Ignacio Miranda

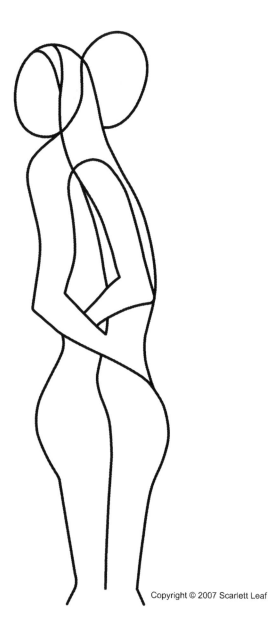

A Tale

Once upon a time, not too long ago, in a charming village near the sun drenched coast of a far off land a most attractive young maiden received an invitation for a special event. On this day, in a quaint little bistro in the center of town, a promising 'weaver of words' would be reading from his latest creation. Intrigued by the notion of meeting someone that may one day become a famous author, she decided to attend.

When she entered the bistro, the proprietor, who was a friend of her family, greeted her warmly. It was at that precise moment, though presently engaged in a conversation with others, that the fair maiden drew the attention of the aspiring writer. Not daring to allow his impulsive imagination to entertain any false hope that she would feel the same towards him, he quickly convinced himself that she was surely beyond his reach. Yet for one moment, her presence completely captivated him. All that his eyes could absorb, all that his senses could detect held him spellbound. Her long silky hair, the playful sparkle in her eyes, her warm smile, her blue dress and the way it clung to her soft shape, her graceful walk and the enticing scent of her cologne that hung in the air—everything about her delighted him.

It was then that the proprietor, a jolly and enthusiastic chap, introduced the young beauty to the handsome writer. She greeted him with her radiant smile and held out her hand to him. Their eyes met, and he gently took hold of the softest and most delicate hand he had ever held. In that moment time stood still and it seemed that, they were the only two people in that room. As much as he wanted to stop the festivities and concentrate only on her, he reluctantly returned his attention to his guest.

Soon the time had come to begin the reading and our excited proprietor wasted little effort moving throughout the crowded room directing everyone to take a seat. Finding a vacant chair near our writer, the maiden joined the group and prepared to listen to his latest masterpiece. Entertaining a few more questions before starting he jovially continued talking with his new friends, all the while hearing her voice above all others when she spoke, and feeling the attraction of her presence through any excitement that the group was generating. The more he listened to her, the more he learned, and the one thing he discovered, the knowledge of which made his heart soar, was that her heart belonged . . . to no one.

This alone brought the impossible within reach again. Nevertheless, what soon followed may have changed the course of history or at least the span of this story as it concerns our aspiring writer. Spurred by the passionate words of his writing, he turned his body slightly in the direction of the fair maiden and began to read. Every word, every syllable found its mark. Her fascination grew with every passage, and just as the sound of his last word dissolved in midair, she uttered her own, a response every writer longs to hear, but one that he especially reveled in from a woman who had captured his heart: "That was beautiful."

Immediately something from within his soul reacted and he knew without question that he had met someone very, very special. It wasn't a matter of what she said or even how she said it although each played its part. It was like magic. Hearing her say those words, knowing that she had made a connection to his writing, only confirmed what he had hoped for from the moment he saw her: that she was an answer to his prayers, the very image of his desires. What he felt for her was more than any words could express, louder than any voice could speak, and sweeter than any song ever sung.

Thus, from that day forward, our beautiful maiden and handsome writer began their love affair. It was a love like no other, which grew beyond their greatest expectations, even beyond comparison to the happiest of fairytales and legends. Now we must leave our lovers in the midst of their tale. Except this story is, as many others are... to be continued.

Just Whisper

Just whisper…
    and I will hear
Just think…
    and I will know
Just call…
    and I will answer
Just ask…
    and I will do
Just want…
    and I will give
Just believe…
    my words are true
Just whisper…
    I love you

Invigorated Love

Revised scene from romance novel 50/50 Split

Calmness began to surface as he felt Suzy's backside nestled close to his arm. Now fully awake, he turned and as he rolled over his face came to rest onto her hair. Soothed by its softness and stirred by its aroma, he closed his eyes and inhaled. Their recent lovemaking came rushing back to his mind in vivid detail. His heart began to beat faster as he moved closer to her. He pressed his frame tightly against hers. Gently, so as not to awaken her, he placed a hand on her hip. Guided by familiarity, his strong fingers followed the path of lingering perspiration from her neck down the valley of her back, and into the firm divide of her buttocks.

Sensing that his midnight touch was not an intrusion, he reached for a bottle of body oil on the nightstand. Pouring some into his palm, Michael rubbed both hands together to warm the cold oil. Starting on the round shape of her shoulder, he worked his hands over the contours of Suzy's sides in smooth, methodical strokes. Feeling her soft skin under his hands made it difficult to restrain from waking her, from engaging her—from thrusting his legs in between hers. Instead, he continued to explore every inch of her exposed body. Up and down, back and forth he intensified each stroke along the areas he knew so well.

As the moments passed, his touch took effect, causing faint moans to escape from Suzy's every breath. Carefully, Michael rose to his knees, where he more thoroughly massaged her sensitive regions. Unconsciously or instinctively, she rolled completely onto her stomach, which encouraged his continued exploration. With each stroke, each tantalizing rub, Suzy echoed her increasing pleasure with deeper moans.

Michael and Suzy's raw desire took them soaring to a climax in a heat of lustful words and invigorated passion; repeatedly, at two am, they confirmed their love for one another.

Roses and Bubbles

Hello Beautiful,

I am so looking forward to this evening with you. Though I should wait until your arrival let me whet your appetite, just a little, with a small sample of what's planned.

First, from the moment you step through the door my arms will embrace you as if for the very first time. My parched lips will then drink from your lips until they thirst no more – this could go on for some time. I'll escort you to a nearby chair. Once seated I'll kneel down, place my hand behind your calf and with my other hand around your ankle slowly raise it slightly off the floor; then tenderly remove your shoe. Soon you will feel the warmth of my hands rubbing your entire foot meticulously working my fingers in, while massaging the stress of the day out. Afterwards, your other leg will receive the same warm soothing rubs. However, before you slip into blissful contentment I'll stop so that I can lead you down the hallway.

We'll stop in front of a closed door and I'll ask you to close your eyes. Once I'm satisfied that you're not peeking, because I know how you are, I'll open the door and immediately you'll be greeted by the most delicate scents you can imagine. The sweet smell of fresh cut roses co-mingled with the enticing lure of aromatic oils will tempt you to open your eyes, when you'll behold a romantic display of beauty and enchantment. At that time, before the alluring fragrances can capture your senses, with the flick of a switch I'll add the instrumental sounds of smooth jazz music to this dreamy ambiance.

Hand in hand, you and I will walk on a cool tiled floor covered with red rose petals. Along the way, the soft glow of a dozen candles will appear to dance in your honor. At the end of the floral path will be a closed pair of deep purple curtains. I'll tie them back to reveal your private Oasis: a spacious tub brimming over with a cloud-like latte of a million tiny bubbles. Scattered about the bubbly veil like red cherubs are more flower petals some of which will find their way onto the granite surface that surrounds your retreat. More scented candles and two crystal bowls are at the foot of the tub. One, filled with rich creamy chocolates and the other with sweet juicy strawberries.

I'll pull you close and help you prepare: my hands will slide along your waist until I reach the back of your skirt. Patiently, I'll find that illusive single clasp. With your zipper between my fingertips, with my lips against your ear, your skirt will fall to the floor. Afterwards, while I gaze into your eyes my hands will move to the front of your blouse and one by one, each button unfasten, each strap undone until nothing else remains. Finally, after I stop caressing your hair, squeezing your body and kissing your lips, I'll help you into this hot sudsy dream.

I'll sit on the edge of the tub and hand you a long stemmed glass from the nearby counter filled with your favorite wine. We'll laugh, drink and talk about all the interesting events of your day. Amid our lighthearted conversation without notice, I plan to reach into the water and take hold of your leg. Gently, I'll lift it above the suds and begin stroking up and down its entire length till finally, at some point, turn my attention to your foot. With just the right amount of pressure my massage will travel from your heel through your sole and on into each individual toe. This could go on for some time. Placing your leg back beneath the water my focus will shift to the other leg where again apply my special touch. While I massage your toes, I think I'll play a little game which may cause you to giggle and laugh. "This little piggy went to market and this little piggy stayed home and this little piggy…" and so on until I come to the last of five which I'll proceed to say something like… "And this little piggy," I'll pause for effect, "And this precious little piggy… needs a kiss." With that being said, I'll lean down and affectionately kiss your toe.

Well, I've disclosed more than perhaps I should, but of course, there's more in store. Except I will offer one more detail. Right before I leave you to enjoy your special "me" time I mean to press my month onto yours and give you the most passionate kiss that my lips and tongue can produce. Afterwards, when I'm finally able to pull myself away from you I will disappear into the kitchen where I will prepare a special dinner for two.

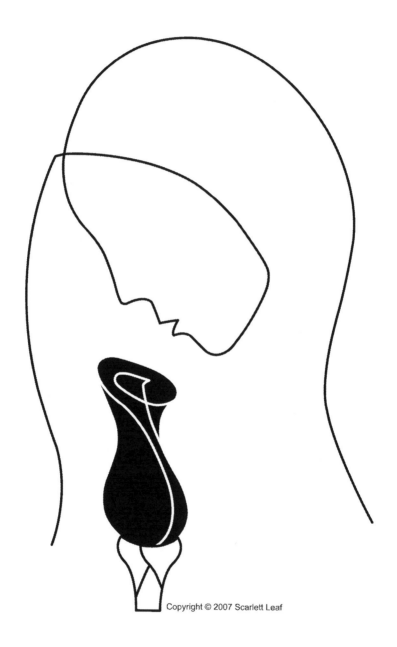

My Favorite Flower

Oh, the beauty and splendor which soil thus yields
From the lowest of valleys to the highest of hills
Every nation and culture through history has known
A sweet floral display which nature has shown

Mmmm, something about flowers engages my senses. Whether it's giving a colorful bouquet or a single bud; strolling leisurely through meadows of wild flora or seeing flowers displayed in the simple containers of a road side stand, to be in the presence of nature's gift is always an incredible experience. As you can tell, I love flowers. They are exquisite representatives of creation's beauty and wonder. For centuries, flowers have been a vital part of the human experience. They soothe and comfort, they arouse and excite. Many are edible with nutritional and medicinal properties. From mud huts in the most remote parts of the world to the magnificent palaces of Kings and Queens in the wealthiest of nations, all people of every culture have always held flowers in high regard.

How blessed we are with such a seemingly endless variety of shapes, sizes and colors. Perhaps most incredible of all are the distinctive fragrances of the varied species. What a delight it is to be in a meadow on a warm spring day lying on a blanket spread over a bed of soft green grass. Your eyes drift up into a clear blue sky. High above, puffy white clouds slowly drift by while in a nearby tree a pair of doves coos. Your eyes close as a gentle breeze co-mingled with the sweet scent of Jasmines whispers its scent. On the other hand, imagine sitting in a quiet place sipping a cup of hot herbal tea and observing the delicate elegance of Orchids. Caressing your ears, the tranquil notes of meditative music float into your soul. Your spirit refreshed by the soothing sounds of a waterfall cascading into a Koa pond. Somewhere between serenity and harmony, your mind floats away. This is bliss.

With all that I've attempted to describe and as much as I love all flowers if I had to choose just one as my favorite, it would have to be a rose. Ever regarded for its sensuous fragrance, graceful shape and its romantic appeal a rose is like no other flower. Moreover, of all the varieties to select from there are three colors that have a special meaning to me.

First, the white rose. White symbolizes purity, kindness, innocence, and peace. It also represents faith, truth and new beginnings, for this reason the flower of choice for coronations, the birth of babies and especially when two become one, as in a wedding, is the rose.

Then there is the yellow rose. The vibrant color yellow fosters joy, optimism, creativity, courage, wisdom and enthusiasm. Universally recognized as the color that represents friendship it also conveys hope as with the displaying of yellow ribbons for the homecoming of loved ones.

Then there is the splendor of the red rose. Widely known as the flower of romance and love just the color alone stimulates one's senses. For red represents passion, energy, power, desire, strength and vitality. It is no small wonder that a red rose conveys such a powerful message.

Yet, with all that I attempted to portray there is an exception. One flower comes to mind that, for me, makes all that I've described seem like mere after thoughts. One so beautiful and so rare, so delicate yet ever so vibrate and resilient, a flower so special that the creation of a unique category would be appropriate. Because you see that flower which I speak of... is you. Therefore, it is fair to say that you truly are *My Favorite Flower*.

For these reasons, *My Favorite Flower*, I give to you the following: A white rose for you are truly pure in heart, generous in deed and selflessly kind. Moreover, because of you I embraced a new beginning... with you, I learned how to breathe again, how to live again... how to sing and dance again.

Next, I give you a yellow rose because you see, like no other, your enthusiasm excites me and your courage inspires me. Admittedly, sometimes your insights challenge me; nevertheless, there is no doubt in my mind that I chose well when I selected you as my confidant. Never before have I ever felt more at ease or more inclined to share with someone my most guarded inner feelings than I do with you. Truly, you are my dearest of friends

Last, but by no means least, I give to you a red rose. What can I say: if red represents passion, energy, vitality, and desire then let this red rose signify what you mean to me, because with you I have experienced intimacy and romance as I never knew existed. With you I have tasted, I have felt and I have loved far beyond my wildest expectations. I never knew I could love anyone as much as I love you *My Favorite Flower.*

With All

I will love you

With all my heart
With all my soul
With all... and so much more

With all that I am
And with all that I aspire to be
With each new day
When fast asleep each night

I will love you

With hope, joy and laughter
With passion for every desire
With a conviction that is true
With patience that is long
With words that comfort and ears that hear
All the days ahead whether good or bad
And the nights we spend making amends

I will love you

Your Song

(a Ballad)

I just want to know
Do you know what true love is?

For me it's like… having this dream
Where I never let you go

And I want you to know…
If I could, this I would do
I'd take you into my arms
And make love to you
Like you never seen
Like you only dreamed

Every time I look in your eyes
I see the beauty of your soul

You've become so special to me
More precious than… diamonds and gold

Baby you need to know
If I could, this I would do
I'd take you into my arms
And make sweet love to you
Oh–if you would try
And let yourself go
I'd take you into my arms
And never let you go
Oh–if I could
I… would… take… you, into my arms.
And make love to you
Like you never seen
Like you only dreamed

Asleep in My Arms

It was mid October. The day's bright sunrays had long passed their appointed time and in their place, pale beams of an autumn moon tapped on our windowpanes in the clear night sky. Alone for the first time, we sat together sipping wine and laughing throughout the night. I remember it so clearly: The twin wingback chairs with blue silky cushions and between us that little mosaic table with a beveled glass. Then, in the midst of our light-hearted atmosphere came an abrupt silence. Still smiling, we each looked away; embarrassed at the chemistry we were starting to feel, feelings unexpectedly discovered. It was at that very moment that I felt this urgent need, this sudden compulsion to listen to my heart and act upon it, but I wasn't sure I could or should.

My tongue would not obey me and I stammered, almost speechless. I tried to clear my throat, but this was of little help. I tried to appear calm, and I hoped you could not sense my turmoil. How do I convey my true feelings to you? My palms began to sweat, and I clenched the arms of the chair, half rubbing my palms on the fabric to dry them. Despite my uncertainty, I could not quell this strong sensation emanating from within my heart. Sensing that it was now or never, I leaned forward, looked into your eyes, and sang you a song—"Your Song," as I later dubbed it.

Slow in tempo with short phrasings and simple words, it was an uncomplicated song, and I sung it more or less in tune. More importantly, the song represented what was deep in my heart.

After the last note had trailed away, I smiled and quietly awaited your response, all the while wishing I had the titillating vocals of a Michael Bublé or the lyrical styling of a Smokey Robinson or the seductive smoothness of Luther Vandross.

Without applause or fanfare, you stood up and tossed your coat on the chair. I watched you walk across the room towards the bed. I sat in eager anticipation, not knowing your intentions. The lines of your shape and your curves seemed drawn to perfection; the sway of your stride, the graceful swing of your arms, and the swish of your hair were stunning. I thought to myself oh, how I love to see you come, but mmmm, how I love to see you go.

You stood near the bedside table holding a paisley printed gift bag. From it, you placed a lovely candle arrangement set in an oval-shaped glass bowl on the table. You lit the candles, and afterwards you switched off a nearby lamp. Soon the arousing scent of Jasmine and Roses filled the air. You paused. You turned. As you turned around you swept your hair over your shoulder, smiled and slowly moved toward me. I so enjoyed the thrill of the unexpected your silence suggested but even more by what I hoped you smile hinted. With each step the soft glow of dancing candlelights, seem to follow your every movement. As you approached, my heart began beating faster and faster and before I knew what was happening—you climbed into my lap. You drew close to me and effortlessly settled on top of me, molding your body to mine. Without thought, my hand strayed to the rise of your hip and I held you to me. Having you this close to me, I could not think, I could not move, for I was in total awe. We held each other's gaze without a sound—who needed words?

Eyes fastened, and bodies entwined, our souls became one in the revelation of a mystery we could never have predicted. I knew then that if I had to spend the rest of all eternity with only one precious image, the memory of that moment would be with me forever.

Drifting further into this peaceful state, I noticed your eyes gradually began to close. As I watched the slowing tempo of your breathing, I felt a slight nudge from your legs—followed by the soft thud of shoes hitting the floor. Looking down I was strangely drawn to your feet—they were smooth and supple from heel to toe. After gazing at their perfect symmetry for what seemed like hours; I closed my eyes and I realized you felt weightless upon me, as soft as a cloud, and endearing as a dream.

Imagine, if you will, wrapped in a single space of time the euphoria you feel with birthdays, Christmases and all pleasant things. This is how I felt, holding the one I quietly have always loved. Slowly I tilted my head up opened my eyes and finally looked back at your face, only to discover that you had fallen asleep. In my arms, lay a vision of pure beauty. I was star struck, mesmerized, enthralled and every other expression I could use to describe how I felt as I looked at you.

Forgive my clumsy words, but words are useless to express how I feel about you. Holding you like never before I looked at you, with your eyelashes curled in sweet slumber, your lips ever so slightly parted, and concealing your cheek—a lock of hair. I swept it away and spied your diamond stud earring glimmering with each breath you took. Your hands, so lovely, laid against my chest… touched my heart. I could hardly believe this was happening. Had I fallen asleep? Was this a dream? I could no longer restrain myself. I leaned my head down and caringly pressed my lips against yours. Slowly I raised my head—you smiled. I realized at that moment that you truly care for me, and I felt the way you trusted me, asleep in my arms was your way of saying, "I love you."

Love Softly Spoken

April morning
Tan leather jacket, fitted blue jeans
Yes, I remember
First hello, hours on the phone
Through laughter and tears
A secret revealed, dreams shared
Passion began to kindle

Awkward moments of our first date
Would this be the last?
Dare I call, dare I not
How else could I be sure?
Call, concerns, all laid to rest
The moment I heard "Hello"

Watching sunsets by the sea
Wishing on a star
Sharing food, a single plate
Each glass of Cabernet
Cuddle together, a king size blanket
Greet the rising sun

Slow dance, warm summer night
Brushing back your hair
Gently caress your soft sweet face
Lips passionately pressed
Together, never enough
Apart, far too long
Eyes fasten
Hearts throb
Love softly spoken

Passing Thoughts

Not sure when it all began. Was it at the first hello? Was it the first time I touched your hand?

On the other hand, could it have been at that moment when I first looked into your eyes. Perhaps it all started the instant I first kissed your lips. Even though I cannot say with certainty, this I do know. Whenever it began—a love began, that has no end

ⵕ ⵕ

Long before our love grew true
Prior to our hearts, delight
Soon after when we first met
A time before that kiss goodnight
You and I were friends

ⵕ ⵕ

There are those times when I wish I could go an entire day… without thinking about you… without wanting you, without needing you. So far, that wish has not come true.

More Thoughts

No other breath—will do
No other smile—will do
No other lips—will do
Unless they all belong to you

 CB &0

I remember the first hello and the last good-bye, the tireless walks and our endless talks, each gentle touch and every soothing embrace: warm summer nights with stars so bright and the clean brisk air of an early morning hike: wining and dining and dancing till dawn, window shopping just for fun and exploring the wonders of eclectic art forms, through laughter and tears and the deep secrets we shared, ooh the passion we experienced when we were together—I remember it all.

CB &0

No matter your mood... it's always refreshing to be with you.
No matter what you wear... it's always classy and refined.
No matter what you say... it's always cheerful and uplifting.
No matter the time of day... it's always a delight to be with you.

Surrender

Revised scene from romance novel 50/50 Split

Driven by a passion he could barely contain, Spencer turned and pinned Suzy against the door of an executive suite. Griping both of her hands, words of romance flowed from his lips. He spoke of the wonders of her beauty, the allure of her charm, and the passion he felt for her. With their eyes locked, each phrase he spoke drew them closer together. Outwardly, he was cool and composed, but within, nervous expectation raged. The enticing contour of her slightly open mouth enhanced by flaming red lipstick, and a hint of gloss, beckoned his every masculine desire.

Each word whispered drew their lips firmly and completely together. Then out of nowhere to Spencer's shocked, Suzy pulled her lips away like a thief caught in an awful crime as a look of disbelief enveloped her face. "No, no… this isn't right. We can't. I can't. I'm married!"

In spite of her weak pleas neither one was willing to let go of the other. Her vain words of rejection diminished with each syllable until can't became can. As they stood, unashamed, in each other's embrace, Spencer sprang the key card from his pocket. He inserted it into the lock with smooth precision. As he pushed the door open with his foot, he all but carried her into the room.

Ecstasy Suzy never before imagined transcended her wildest erotic fantasy. The scent of his Gucci cologne lulled her deeper into submission, permitting Spencer to work the zipper down the back of her dress. She squeezed her arms into the strength of his well-defined back and wildly raked her fingers through his soft hair. With their bodies firmly pressed together, she began to feel the growing firmness of Spencer's loin. Suzy's grip tightened.

Between passionate kisses and the journey his hands sought over her body, he blazed a trail with his tongue between her neck and her ears. Repeatedly, Spencer poured irresistible words into her ears ripping away the last remnants of inhibition. Piece by piece, her dress fell to floor, followed by his clothes until all that remained was a littered pathway. The path ended at a closed door. Caught beneath it, Suzy's black laced panties… the last shred of her faithfulness… the ending struggle between can't and can.

Once More

Hello,

My room is dark and cold. My thoughts are replete with despair. My life has no meaning.

Though more days than I care to remember have come and gone, the only connection I can seem to make between denial and reality comes from your last words spoken, "I've given up on us being together."

Well I too have given up except I fear I've given up on me. At times, I feel as though I am standing on the outside looking at a discarded caricature of myself. I don't shave. I don't brush my teeth. I just don't care.

Slipping into another such episode something from deep within compels me, perhaps out of sheer survival to write to you and express my feelings. Even though you may never read my letter I must write it if for no other reason than to relieve my sorrow – confront the truth.

Looking back, I'm dumbfounded that I offered no resistance or try to refute your decision. Even stranger to me is the fact that, though outwardly I may have appeared cordial and accommodating, is inwardly my mind went into shock. I felt so numb and lifeless. I could not think or speak. Nevertheless, I wish I had done more than simply watch you walk away.

Fighting hard to be objective, I had to put an end to my self-imposed torture and discard all the "what-ifs" that besieged me. I had to stop condemning my efforts to prove that we belong together, that my love was different. Then again, I can now see how my zeal and impatience had been at times too intense, even to the point of smothering. Instead of nurturing our relationship, I was forcing it. What a paradox, I was both developing and undermining the very thing I wanted most of all… a lasting and loving relationship with you.

I remember those nights; you shared with me your pains and the disappointments, the lies, the deceptions, and the struggles you had endured from passed relationships. Yet, I did not understand the depth of their consequences or the measures you had taken to guard your heart. Because of this, I must confess, I was unprepared.

Looking back, I clearly recall signs you gave and comments you made pertaining to patience except my arrogance and pride did not yield. I really believed, eventually, you would see it my way. Yet, how could I in all fairness to you have expected this? How could I have insisted that you understand the depth of my commitments when you weren't sure if men were capable of such?

I should have been wiser and exercised more sensitivity regarding your wants and your needs. Had I realized this, I would have seen that in your heart of hearts you hoped that what I offered was real, and that for a time you willingly opened your heart to me. Regrettably, I moved too fast, which fostered more doubts than assurances. Your defenses began to rumble and quake—you ran for cover and consequently, withdrew those emerging feelings for me.

Oh how I wish I could wind back time and do it all over again… if I could only have one more chance to prove my love is true. If you would only try once more to see that, I would offer you a love without measure… a love without conditions… a love that would never end.

So I must ask, will you try once more?

Why Aren't You Here
(a Ballad)

Every time I think of you
I feel this pain
Every time I close my eyes
They start to cry
Ever I look in the mirror
Ask myself why

Why aren't you here?
Why aren't you here?

Lonely days and sleepless nights
Are what you left me
Dusty pictures on the wall
Of fading memories
Every time fall down and pray
My God… why?

Why aren't you here?
Why aren't you here?
Oh-ooh, oh-ooh
Why aren't you here?
Why… aren't you… here?

Loved and Lost

To Whom It May Concern:

In the eighteen hundreds English poet Alfred Lord Tennyson wrote, "Better to have loved and lost than never to have loved at all," On a number of occasions I've offered this phrase as a means of comfort to those that lost a loved one. Not necessarily, the kind of love lost associated with death, but rather the humiliating distress that plagues a person who suffers from rejection by the one they love. How easy it had been for me to console someone with such advice when my own affairs were intact. However, when it's me drowning in sorrow, oh how difficult it is to heed the advice I once so cavalierly gave.

With drapes drawn shut I sit in a darkened room clueless as to whether it is day or night. With the phone turned off, clock covered over and the remains of discarded flowers on the floor I sit miserably alone, yet not completely alone. In my solitude, there is a lingering presence. The relentless question remains wedged in my mind: "Is it better to have loved and lost, than to have never loved at all?"

Unable to rid my mind of this intruder I had little choice but to face it. With the only light glaring from my computer screen, I decided to sojourn out of my despair hoping that writing would offer some resolution. Staring at a blank screen my peripheral vision reminds me of the room's vacancy. Though the furnishings remain the same, and the color schemes haven't changed the room is totally empty of meaning or purpose. Gone is the laughter that once reverberated so freely. Gone is the sweet fragrance that once filled the air. Gone is the touch that made everything come alive. Gone are the warmth of smiles, the sparkling eyes and the endless conversations. Gone is the passion that rang through the night. Gone are the promises that accompanied each new morning. It all went away the day you declared we could no longer be together.

So I asked myself is it better for me to have loved and lost only to suffer as I do to hurt as I do? On the other hand, would my life have been better off if I had never known you… if I had never held you… if I had never kissed you… if I had never needed you?

How can I ever listen to music again without thinking of you? How can I go to familiar places and not miss you? It's even difficult to drive my own car knowing I won't have you sitting next to me venturing off to new and exciting places. It's tormenting to go out in public because in every woman I see. I see you. Every sweet fragrance I breathe. I inhale you. Every soft voice I hear, I hear you. Everyday I wish. I wish for you.

The act of writing is fascinating because it helps to release thoughts and emotions desperately needing confronting. For that reason, I must give answer to the question, "Is it better for me to have loved you only to lose you, than never to have loved you at all?" My answer is a resounding "Yes"! Even though I hurt, more than I never knew was possible. Even though I long for and pray for something that may never be. Still. Because of you, I learned to breathe, to live and to love, as I never thought that I could. Because of you words like amazing, beautiful, exciting, fulfilling, passionate, and faithful have a completely new meaning. Because of you, I discovered me. Therefore, I can honestly say because of you my life will never be the same and for this, I am forever grateful.

Never Let You Go
Revised excerpt from romance novel 50/50 Split

I Stanza

As day needs night, and night needs day for seasons to know their
time.
Like a melody needs a musician for notes to come alive.
To know you are there when I sleep, and will be there when I awake.
As the stars need the heavens and the sky needs the color blue.
Being that breath needs air, flowers need rain, and Adam needed Eve
Just like yesterday needs today so there will be a tomorrow... I need
you.

II Stanza

In truth, I would wish that our break up had never happened,
That it was all a misfortunate dream... but in fact, it did.
Though I would never have believed,
I would ever experience life without you... well in fact I did.
To pretend like this whole episode never occurred,
To move on as if it never happened would in fact... be a lie.
By way of loneliness and pain, I have gained a much clearer
perspective,
A far better understanding than I could have ever imagined,
Of how much you mean to me.
Those days those nights those times without you,
Made me realize... I should have fought for you

Never Let You Go

III Stanza

God said it is not good for man to be alone so He gave as a gift... a
wife.
To love, honor, cherish and protect... and let no one come between.
In sickness and in health for richer or for poorer for better or for
worst,
A promise to keep always
A vow I may not have broken, yet to know and practice not,
May be a far worst offence.
Overall when I think back over those days when I sum it all up when
I explore it
When I examine it when I finally admit the truth...
I should have fought for you

IV Stanza

In my fear of losing I held on so tight, I nearly squeezed the life from
you.
Through my selfishness, I refused to hear, because of ignorance I
refused to know.
What is more, with my stubborn pride I gambled away you who
mattered most.
Instead of nurturing, I withheld, therefore starving you of your
potential.
When I should have given I was busy taking, thus I devalued your self
worth.
A day without your smile... a night without your kiss... a life
without your touch...
Is more than I can bear.
I should have fought for you... I should have never let you go

How Much

Words alone cannot proclaim
Paper stacked high can never contain
Volumes of books will never explain
How much you mean to me

My mind will not submit to rest
Until my heart can fully express
What other bards have quoted best
How much you mean to me

I pondered for the longest time
Each word I struggled to refine
So you would know without restraints
How much you mean to me

It needs to be clear devoid of a twist
Please understand if my words are a mist
After all that's been said, it comes down to this…

More than
Fortune and fame
The air I breathe
The sustenance for my body
Than all my hopes and deepest desires

You mean that much to me

A Note

Oh my love,

Last night, no matter how hard I tried I could not fall asleep. Though my mind knew it was time to rest, my heart would not stop replaying those treasured moments we shared. Standing, embracing and kissing beneath a canopy of lightly scattered clouds and dazzling heavenly lights was like living a dream. The ebb and flow of waters splashing against our feet, accompanied by the cascading sounds of an aquatic recitation seemed to stimulate sensuous and rhythmic movements of your body against mine. If not for the cool breeze that swirled around our entwined bodies the heat between us might have spawned, on that secluded beach, a night of unrestrained pleasure.

As I lay, somewhat content with only images of you, my arms invariable take hold of a pillow in a vain attempt to recapture the contours of your soft warm body. I recalled the floral scent of your cologne "Happy" and the way it lay on your skin; now it lingered on my pillow, and caused every cell of my body to repeatedly call out for you. Each image was only a sample of the intoxication I felt from the taste of your sweet delicate lips. My eyes, though closed, could clearly see deep into your beautiful eyes—eyes that beckoned me, enraptured me, and soothed my soul.

Everything about you moves me, stirs me, and intrigues me like no one I have ever known before. Though I spend hours and sometimes days with you, it never seems to be enough. I never ever want our time together to end. Oh sweet love, you have become an important part of my life. With you, my dreams have come true; in fact, you far exceed my wildest dreams and hope-filled expectations. You, my precious love, are a gift sent from heaven—a gift, I believe, reserved just for me.

A Woman is a Gift

Good morning Beautiful,

Last night I had the most incredible dream, unlike any dream I've ever had. It was so real and so beautiful I just had to share it with you.

I dreamt that in the beginning after the creation of the heavens and earth and all living things that I was the first human. Formed from the dust of the earth I was a one-of-a-kind specimen. However, my form just lay there on the ground stiff and lifeless. Suddenly, from the mouth of God, a breath of warm air began to stream into each nostril. Down through my windpipe swirling molecules of life filled the chambers of my lungs. At that very moment, I became a living soul—I became a man.

Soon after, I found myself in the most spectacular garden one can imagine. It's hard to describe the vibrant colors or the refreshing scents or the natural beauty that abounded. All around animals of every description freely roamed throughout the breath taking landscapes. The air was pure, the blue sky was brilliant and the waters of bubbling springs sparkled like precious jewels. In every direction, this glorious paradise had no limits or boundaries. Even a cool breeze that rustled through the tree leaves sounded like music... such peace... such harmony.

So there I was happily living in a slice of heaven and while no one else existed, interestingly, I never felt lonely. I remember walking through a meadow, and even though I was not tired, I felt compelled to lie down on a grassy knoll beneath the shade of huge tree. As I began to fall asleep, I thought I heard a soft voice almost like a whisper say, "It is not good for man to be alone. Therefore I will make for him a helper, someone compatible with him."

Soundly asleep, I was oblivious to everything except a kind of intrinsic awareness that something truly monumental was taking place.

(I was certainly unaware that being removed from my chest a rib bone.) Then once again I heard the same voice but now it was unmistakably speaking directly to me, "Awake man, for I have a special gift just for you."

Gradually my eyes opened and posed before me was a brilliant light that glistened like ribbons of pure gold. With each blink of my eyes, which seem to move in slow motion, layer after layer of splendor gracefully began to reveal the contours of a very shapely silhouette. The anticipation caused emotions to surge through me unlike anything I had never experienced before. I then sat up and with both hands rubbed my eyes in an attempt to quicken my ability to focus. As I removed my hands, I could not believe my eyes. It's difficult to put into words the full magnitude of that moment. If I could have taken every flower of the world and every precious gem that ever was. To gather all the grandeur of a sunrise and the splendor of a sunset, if it were at all possible to harvest the brilliance of every star in the heavens and assemble all things good, all things sweet and all things lovely, gracious and pure, it could not come close to describing the vision my eyes beheld. For nothing before or anything since compares to the gift that I was given and that gift I speak of was you.

My heart's pounding was so intense that my right hand reached for my chest. I don't know how but the instant my hand touched my side I knew a vital part had gone from me, that the Master Designer of all had lovingly used it to fashioned you. Everything about you was perfect. From the crown of your elegant hair to the soles of your pretty feet; with each curve of your sensuous body to the glow of your smooth skin up to your sweet angelic face, all radiated with pure loveliness. Your gorgeous eyes gazed at me with deep affection, your loving smile welcomed me, your extended arms beckoned me and from your sweet voice I heard, "Embrace me my love."

Instantly I leaped to my feet, and with unrestrained joy and excitement rushed into your waiting arms. We held each other so tightly. We kissed each other so fervently. We loved each other so completely. Our hearts began to beat as one—I kissed your ear tenderly and whispered, "You my love… are flesh of my flesh and bone of my bone. We shall be as one, always and forever."

Then, in the middle of our embrace in the heat of the moment, I woke up. I tried to go back to sleep and recapture my dream, but I couldn't. Consequently, I simply lay there and thought, was this merely a case of imaginary fantasy or was there more to it? Was there a hidden meaning an encrypted message that I needed to understand? For an entire day, I couldn't stop thinking about it until finally the dream made sense: A woman is a gift and you, my love, are a gift to me.

In my dream as in real life, I was content but not complete. I believe by divine design you are the perfect complement and my ideal companion. Your compassion, kindness, and friendship comfort and console me. Your intellect, sensitivity, and intuitions advise me. Your respect, confidence, and admiration strengthen me. Your love, your passion and your touch invigorate me. I can honestly say you bring out the best in me.

I now understand why you were fashioned from my rib, because you are to be the closest person to my heart. Moreover, when you consider that the heart of a man is vulnerable your perspectives and discernments are invaluable to my interest. How fascinating it is to know you were selected from the closest part of my being—my heart. This would explain how it is that you know me so well, literally, from the inside out.

Though we are equals, we are yet uniquely different which makes us a wonderful match. Where I am weak, you are strong and vice versa. If I am down your spirit lifts me up. When my enterprising zeal advances at the speed of sound, you wisely caution me. How is it that a single word of encouragement from you has more impact on me than a thousand words from anyone else? I'm convinced that with our combined individual attributes, together we can work toward any goal, conquer any obstacle and flourish in any endeavor.

So my love may I restate once more and say you are so special; deserving of my honor and my praise: deserving of my trust and my respect: deserving of my loyalty and my commitment. My love, I will laugh with you and cry with you: I will explore with you: and I will grow old with you. I will always be here for you. This I seal with all my heart, with all my soul, with all my being and most of all, with all my love. Yes, I do understand that a woman is a gift and you my precious love are truly a heavenly gift to me.

Come To Me

Come to me
Oh, my love
Inhale
Sweet enticement
Rest your head
Upon my chest
Let love have its way tonight

Kiss my ears
The way you do
Free
The passion within
Kiss my lips
Again and again
Let love have its way tonight

Press your body
Against mine
Cover me
With your scent
Appease my tongue
Tasting your skin
Let love have its way tonight

Lay between
Sheets of love
Touching
Moving
Pleasing
Each other completely
Let love have its way tonight

Kailua Cream

When I was young, I dreamed a dream
Of finding my true love
With cheeks so soft and lips so sweet
Her voice was like an angel

Each day her smile would warm my heart
Her touch would soothe my soul
Her eyes so beautiful would gaze into mine
Her embrace would never let go

From the clothes she wore to the texture of her hair
Always pleasing and refined
With love and compassion, wit and charm
A wonderful woman to fine

Though I am older, I still have this dream
'Cause my heart believes it's true
Yet to my surprise the day had arrived
I found my dream in you

So no matter the time whether day or night
My thoughts embrace my dream
And call out your name that is special to me…
My sweet Kailua Cream

Song of Lovers

Expressions of a Married Couple
Inspired by the Book of Solomon

She said; Kiss me with the kisses of your mouth for your love is better than wine.

Let the scent of your cologne draw me near tell me of your feelings.

You, who I yearn, tell me whom do you truly desire?

He said; Don't you know? None compare to you not even precious gems can be compared. Your loveliness surpassed only by your inner beauty and strength. Your countenance, as if adorned with every array of expensive jewels. Just thinking of you ignites my passions and stirs my desires.

She said; Come, close to me and be intoxicated with my love. Inhale my enticing aroma. Come lay all night between my breasts—taste the flavor of my skin.

He said; Lying here held by love the sweet scent of your body fills my breath. As I lie enraptured by your love my nostrils fill with the bouquet of countless rose petals. Come look at me and let me see your lovely face let me hear your sensuous voice let me absorb your studding features. Come to me my gorgeous lover.

She said; Oh my sweet, you are mine and I am yours and I truly value how you honor me how thoughtfully you cover me as with a quilt of love. Cradle me now with your left hand beneath my head. Soothe my appetite by embracing me with your right. For I hunger for your love, I crave your touch and I desire you words.

He said; You my love bring out the best in me. I've never known a woman so captivating, so intriguing, and so passionate. Each time I'm with you, I discover another facet of your loveliness. The softness of your hair, the warmth of your smile and the sensitivity of your touch all appease me. Your sumptuous lips invite my kisses, and the breath of your speech draws me in. In my arms, your body is firm yet to my touch—soft and tender. How wonderful is your love. Beautiful woman your love is better than fine wine and the lure of your scent captivates my senses even a whiff of your garments arouses my emotions. Being with you is like being in a Tropical garden overflowing with delicious fruits, fragrant flowers, and exotic spices accentuated by the tranquil sounds of a fresh water stream.

She said; Oh sweet love, feeling your breath blow upon my garden causes the timbre of my essence to vibrate. Each kiss of your lips inflames my temperature. Etched in my soul is the image of your intense body, covering me as a blanket of love. Come my love into my garden and enjoy the fruits I possess.

He said; Yes my love, I will enter your garden and consume all that you offer. I will eat of your sweetness as though I were eating pure honey. I will drink the liquor of your passion as we rejoice together as one.

She said; To hear you speak this way causes my entire insides to quiver with anticipation.

Speak my love, for your words evoke my deepest fervor. The warmth of your gentle smile and the kindness of your lovely eyes, pierce my soul like no other. Each touch of your fingers reach deep within the very core of my essence. How sensitive you are to my every need and desire. Your strength of character is truly without reproach as though built upon pillars of marble. How I love you so, you are more to me than a lover because you are also my friend.

He said; Sometimes, my lovely woman, when I gaze into your eyes I am so overcome with delight knowing that you are with me. Though there are many women all around there is only one meant for me and that is you. My precious beauty, I adore and appreciate so much about you. The clothes you tastefully wear wonderfully accentuate your femininity. The curves of your belly gracefully meld into the contours of your hips in through your smooth thighs and sculpted calves then coming to rest at your soft tender feet. Rising above your twin breasts are like firmly anchored towers, which beckon my ascent. Moreover, the lines of your neck regally hold your head up so majestically whereupon my eyes become fixated onto your angelic face. For your eyes your lashes your brow your nose your lips your cheeks all so delightfully compliment one another. Most of all your grace, beauty and kindness are only matched by the intellect you posses. You are so beautifully complete and you are so completely mine.

She said; I am yours, your lover and your friend clearly; your desire is only for me.

Come my handsome man, let us go and arouse the night together then rise to the fresh morning of our bed and breathe the fragrant potpourri that sensuously fills our room. Place your left hand beneath my head and let your right arm embrace me. Set me as a seal upon your heart and securely hold me in your arms for our love is strong. Many waters cannot quench our love nor can the floods of 1000 storms drown it. I'm convinced that your love for me is not just for the nights but for all times during all seasons through all circumstances and in all situations. I sincerely believe that our love goes deeper than anyone can imagine further than any eye can see. For I give my all to you and you to me, because we were meant to be.

He said; Precious one, words alone cannot express what you mean to me. I gave you my heart and you locked it away into your soul and wisely hid the key. You touched my inner being and captured my heart long before I came into you. You are mine and I am yours forever and always. My vows, my promises, my commitments are pure and true and are valid to you and to you only. I do love you so, my one and only love.

45

Plain and Simple

Within my heart you will find
No truer love than that of mine
Look close if you will and you will see
The kind of love you hoped could be
I declare today and each day after
My love for you won't fade or falter
Although these words aren't poetically nimble
Sometimes it's best—be plain and simple

Beside a Great Man

Recently, while communing with nature at my favorite Oceanside location, I thought about my life's journey. It was during this time that a familiar phrase came to mind, "Beside every great man is a great woman."

I believe that history, without question, bears witness to this account. When men are accredited with greatness, however one defines greatness, clearly a woman, more often than not, is directly or indirectly involved.

Prompted by the phrase I began to recount the key points of my life—more specifically, the people who have influenced me. Quite honestly, those at the forefront of my thoughts were all women. Now this is not to say that men have not influenced my life; nothing could be further from the truth. Still when I think about it, there is a particular group of women, and each of them in their own way, has had a profound impact on me.

Now first and foremost is my mother. My mom, though a divorced woman of limited means possessed a mindset and a determination that knew no limits. She endured so much and sacrificed for so long in order to give my brother and me a good foundation for manhood. I can remember my mother coming home from a hard day at work, and somehow, having the strength to stay up late and quiz me on my homework. She enrolled us in music classes and sent us to numerous cultural events. She taught us how cook and how to clean the house. Moreover, while I was still in school every summer, thanks to her prompting, I had a paying summer job.

Others correct me if I'm wrong, but I believe my mom was successful in raising her two boys to be men. Even to this day, when we talk she still has much to offer me. As I think back on those childhood days and as certain scenes play out in my mind, I realize that this high regard, this affinity that I have towards women is rooted in those days at home with mom. I suppose this would explain, at least in part, why I feel both compelled and at the same time fulfilled when I write on the subject of love.

Next are my fifth and sixth grade teachers. Even after all these years later, I can still remember their names and clearly see each of their faces. These dear women were the perfect complement for that transitional period from elementary school to secondary school. They were tough and no child that I knew of ever misbehaved in their respected classes. But they were by no means tyrants, and I really enjoyed them and had fun in both classes. Nevertheless, they commanded respect. Of course, back when I was a child, respect for elders and teachers was the norm. However, it was much more than the social standards of the time that made them special, at least for me. Underlying their no-nonsense methods was a sincere passion to instill in us not just lessons and information, but a lifelong desire to learn, to think and to believe that anything is possible. Back in those days, teachers like this guaranteed no child would be left behind. I'm sure that the seeds for creative writing, if not planted, were certainly well nurtured by these dear ladies.

Of course, my opening statement would not be complete without giving high honors to my high school sweetheart, the bride of my youth, and my wife for nearly thirty-three years. Through the many difficulties of every imaginable situation, she stood right there beside me. I have always been a dreamer with high aspirations and even though there were times when she could not see what I envisioned she would cheer for me. And when my endeavors went contrary to plan and I found myself flat on my face, she would help me to my feet, brush me off and kiss away my bumps and bruises.

Starting a marriage as young as we were (would you believe sixteen and seventeen) we obviously had a lot of growing up to do, and fortunately for us in the process grew closer together. Although there was a brief period when our yellow brick road almost did a 50/50 split, thankfully we realized we were much better off together than apart.

Speaking of growing, one area of growth in particular, which I continue to grow into this very day, is to understand the needs and characteristics of a woman. I can remember overhearing a conversation, she had with her girlfriends during which her friends said some nice things about me. You know, all the good stuff a guy likes to be known for. Well, at some point in the exchange of husband niceties before I could puff up my chest, my wife interrupts and humorously replied, "Girls, you just don't know. He wasn't always like this. I've got a lot of time invested in that man." Before long, they were all laughing and I have to admit I laughed along with them.

Then there is the legacy of our union, three daughters and one son. All of them would make their momma, who watches them from heaven, very proud. Moreover, I take great comfort in knowing that through it all from the moment her lips said, "I do," to the instant her spirit said, "good-bye," she loved me... unconditionally.

A short time ago, I met someone with a life story that has become a tremendous source of inspiration, the kind of heroine material for which great books are written and classic movies are made. If ever I need an example to help me embrace life to its fullest, to see the good and beauty in all things and with all that I do have fun, I've been blessed with such a person. Someone that invigorates me, challenges me, calms me and advises me; a woman who many love, respect and admire, a woman who is as intelligent as she is beautiful, as generous as she is enterprising. A woman, I am so privileged to call... my friend.

There you have it—a short-list of the women who have contributed to my life thus far. I can only hope that the nature of my life's work in some way pays homage to women everywhere. For that reason, in closing may I say, "For all that I am and for all that I aspire to be and for whatever measure of greatness that I may possibly receive I attribute to the women who have imparted so much to me, Thank you!"

A Prayer

Dear Heavenly Father,

I humbly come before you to pray a simple prayer for a very special person, a prayer for the one you so dearly love, a prayer for the woman I so passionately love.

Though I have said it many times, I can never thank you enough for that particular day which I believe was fate that brought us together and for allowing our relationship to grow.

Therefore, on bended knees I ask that you continue to watch over her and kindly guide her footsteps each day. Give her strength when she feels weak, give her serenity when she feels confused, give her comfort when she feels pain and daily reassure her that she is never alone. Though she is an amazingly modern woman, may she always be in touch with the innocent, playful and awe-inspired little girl that resides inside.

I ask that you bless every area of her life. Moreover, may the sparkle in her eyes, the warmth of her smile, the pleasantness of her voice, and the soothing effect of her touch ever represent your loving nature. May she be anointed with your love from the crown of her lovely head to the sole of her tender feet. May your grace, favor and mercy always precede her wherever she goes, whatever she does, and whomever she meets.

Dear Lord, this night and every night that follows send your angels to stand guard as she sleeps. Give her a good night's rest full of sweet dreams. Let her awaken to a new day refreshed and rejuvenated. Bless her with joy in the morning, peace throughout the day and contentment during the midnight hours. And Father, if you please, as she sleeps permit one angel to come close to her, lean over and sweetly kiss her upon her cheek and whisper in her ear, "You are loved and highly favored."

Amen

51

What Are You Doing To Me

What are you doing to me?

How is it that I think about you all the time?
Why is it, the moment I leave I immediately start to miss you?
How can the taste of your sweet skin linger in my mouth for days?

When I close my eyes, I see your warm inviting smile.
If I think about anything good, pleasant or beautiful, I think about you.
If a cool breeze whispers pass my ears, I hear your voice.
If I hear the approach of high heels, I turn hoping it is you.
Every time I gaze into your stunning eyes, I just melt.

Why do I hunger for your affection… thirst for your kiss, long for your touch, need your embrace?

I desire to fulfill your every wish.
I am desperate for your love.
I want you near me always.
I yearn for your words.
I require you.
I crave you.

Sweet love.
What are you doing to me?

Love is patient and kind
Love is not jealous, boastful, proud, or rude
Love does not demand its own way
Love is not irritable
And it keeps no record when it has be wronged
Love is never glad about injustice
But rejoices whenever the truth wins out
Love never gives up
Love never loses faith
Love is always hopeful
Love endures through every circumstance
Love will last forever

I Corinthians 13:4-7
(New Living Translation)

About the Artist

Manuel Bernal

Manuel Bernal is a graduate of University of Southern California with a B.A. degree in Fine Arts. He has been actively pursuing his passions as an artist and graphic designer for over 10 years.

The essence of his artworks is the depiction of simplicity, life, nature, the human condition, dreams and love. Influenced by such literary periods as the Renaissance, Romanticism, Realism, Abstract, and Surrealism as well as the inspirational works of: Dali, Picasso, Van Gogh, Kalho, Ballejos, Frazetta and Giger, Bernal's creations are uniquely styled. Many of his pieces have been featured throughout Ventura County in numerous art galleries, private showings and specialty boutiques.

As an entrepreneur, he co-owned *Art of Simplicity*, a greeting card company that featured his designs. Currently, he operates, *Scarlett Leaf,* a graphic designs company that produce specialty products based on his artwork as well as servicing the varied graphic design needs of a growing list of clients.

Manuel Bernal lives in Southern California with his wife Yanine and their son, Aidan.

For further information regarding Manuel Bernal's artwork or his artistic and graphic design services please contact:

Web site: www.scarlettleaf.com
Email: art@scarlettleaf.com

About the Artist

Ignacio Miranda

Ignacio Miranda, a resident of Southern California, holds an AA degree in commercial art from Rio Hondo College and a Bachelors of Art degree from Cal State Fullerton University. However, his abilities as an artist go far beyond textbooks and college degrees. He is a gifted artist and his passion for self-expression is so evident in the various medium used to exhibit his talent. From pencil to ink, from watercolors to colored pencils, Miranda's creations are an eclectic treat to the eyes. His art forms range from animation to graphic designs to portraits to caricatures. With a growing demand for his illustrations by writers of both fiction and children's books, Miranda's art studio is full of activity.

Miranda is an avid reader and enjoys basketball, baseball, bowling and jogging. Another favorite pass time is his visits to art museums where he absorbs inspiration from such masters as Michelangelo and Rembrandt. He also loves spending time with his family and getting involved in his community.

For further information regarding Ignacio Miranda's artwork or his artistic services please email, sunking1@hotmail.com